PRESERVING FOR ALL SEASONS

PRESERVING FOR ALL SEASONS

ANNE GARDON

FIREFLY BOOKS

A FIREFLY BOOK

Published by Firefly Books Ltd. 1999

Text and photographs copyright © 1999 Anne Gardon
Originally published as Délices en Conserve by Editions de l'Homme, 1996.

To avoid spoilage and problems, please use common sense and err on the side of
caution when preserving.

Library of Congress Cataloging-in-Publication Data is available

Canadian Cataloguing-in-Publication Data

Gardon, Anne
Preserving for all seasons

Translation of: Délices en conserve.
Includes index.
ISBN 1-55209-322-0

1. Cookery (Canned foods). 2. Canning and preserving. 3. Jam.
4. Marinades. 5. Condiments. I. Title.

TX603.G3713 1999   641.4'2   C98-932619-5

Published in Canada in 1999 by   Published in the United States in 1999 by
Firefly Books Ltd.   Firefly Books (U.S.) Inc.
3680 Victoria Park Avenue   P.O. Box 1338, Ellicott Station
Willowdale, Ontario   Buffalo, New York
Canada M2H 3K1   USA 14205

Produced by: Denise Schon Books Inc.
Design: Gillian Tsintziras, The Brookview Group Inc.
Editor: Charis Cotter

Printed and bound in Canada by Friesens, Altona, Manitoba

The Publisher acknowledges the financial support of the Government of Canada through the Book
Publishing Industry Development Program for its publishing activities.

DEDICATION

I wish to thank all my friends for their support, and their tastebuds.
I couldn't have made this book without them.
And neither without Mother Nature, so a special thanks to her as well.

CONTENTS

FALL 88

WINTER 136

INTRODUCTION

*T*here was a time, not so long ago, when making preserves was a question of survival. The summer's harvest was carefully stored to provide fruit and vegetables for the winter. If you ran out of strawberry jam or tomatoes in January, you would just have to wait till the next summer to have more. Today we can buy tomatoes in December, strawberries in February and exotic fruits all year long.

So why make preserves? To save money? Not really! Even if you hunt for bargains, buy in large quantities, pick or grow your own fruits and vegetables, once you count the time and energy spent in making preserves and then add the cost of jars and utensils, you will certainly agree with me that store-bought food is more economical.

So, why do I keep making my own preserves?

For pleasure! The pleasure of eating uniquely flavored jams and perfectly seasoned pickles, the pleasure of offering savory gifts for the holidays and of course, the pleasure of making them. Some may find the peeling, cutting, stirring and other mindless tasks of preserving boring: I find them relaxing, meditative, almost zen-like. Making preserves gives me the added satisfaction of knowing the food I eat has been prepared with the best possible care.

I used to be busy like a bee all summer long making preserves for winter. I canned, dried or froze the best of my crops instead of eating them when they were fresh. By August, preserving had become a real chore but I kept at it until late in the fall.

I am smarter now.

I make only my favorite jams and preserve only what I don't consume fresh. I eat my preserves within a few weeks or a few months instead of keeping them for later, as I used to do...as if shelves full of untouched food were my security blanket.

I have also spread my work over 12 months. No more summer rush! After all, preserving is a year-long activity, starting in spring with strawberries and ending late in the winter months with citrus marmalades and other exotic delicacies. I enjoy my more relaxed approach, taking each season's harvest as it comes, whether from my garden or the shelves of my neighborhood grocery store. I now find delight in creating preserves for all seasons.

PRESERVING BASICS

*M*aking preserves is easy if you follow a few simple rules.

CLEANLINESS

All utensils should be clean, kitchen counters free of clutter and all ingredients at hand.

INGREDIENTS

Use only top-quality ingredients. Fruit should be ripe but still firm, vegetables young and tender. Buy or pick only what you can process at one time.

PACKING

Do not fill jars to the top. Always leave 3/4 to 1 1/4 inches (2 to 3 cm) head space. This is especially important when sterilizing filled jars. If packed too tight, the liquid will escape from the jar.

JELLY POINT

Several methods can be used to determine the point at which jam or jelly sets. Take a little of the fruit mixture with a cold metal spoon. Cool slightly and let it drip into the pot. The last drops should run together to form a sheet. Or drop a dollop on a cold saucer and leave to cool slightly. Within minutes, a skin will form on top, which should wrinkle when pressed with a finger. You can also use a candy thermometer, though I do not find them accurate 100 percent of the time. Always remove pot from heat when doing a test.

STERILIZATION

Jars are sterilized before being filled (for jams, jellies and pickles) or after being filled (for apricot and peach halves). Even preserves that are kept in the refrigerator should be placed in sterilized jars.

I sterilize empty jars in the oven. This method is just as good as sterilizing in boiling water and it doesn't turn my kitchen into a Turkish bath. Wash and rinse jars thoroughly and sterilize them for 15 minutes at 375° F (190°C). Boil the flat metal disks for 5 minutes to soften the rubber and get a tight seal. You will know the jars are sealed properly when the dimple on the metal lid is down.

To sterilize filled jars, I use a pressure cooker and follow the instructions provided with it. If you do not have one, put jars in a large pot, cover with water and bring to a boil. To prevent breakage, wrap a tea towel or a dishcloth around the jars. Start timing when the water reaches boiling point. Boil 20 minutes and remove jars with clamps.

CONSERVATION

Keep jars in a cool, dry and dark place, ideally a cold cellar or a basement. Certain kinds of preserves keep better in the refrigerator.

FOOD SPOILAGE

Botulism is caused by spoiled food and it is a very serious illness that can be fatal. After packing the jars, if you notice a few that have not sealed properly, refrigerate them and use them as soon as possible. When properly sealed, the lid should make a popping sound when removed for the first time. If the food looks or smells funny, is mushy, discolored or moldy, discard it immediately. Do not taste it.

QUANTITIES

Preparing too many jars at one time takes all the fun out of making preserves. It also invites sloppiness, which leads to food spoilage. Why spend time preparing tons of food if it is to be thrown away later? Except for a couple of recipes (e.g., Indian chutney), all the preserves in this book can be made in 1 hour or less.

EQUIPMENT

No special equipment is really needed for making jams, although some utensils make preserving easier.

HEAVY POT

I use 2 types of pot. An enamel-coated cast-iron pot is used for simmering jams. It radiates heat evenly and can go into the oven. I also use a 12-quart (12 L) stainless steel pot for pickles, sauces and salsas. Its deep sides help reduce splashing.

PRESSURE COOKER

Call me old-fashioned but if I were given a choice between a pressure cooker and a microwave oven, I would certainly choose the first. A microwave is great for defrosting or reheating prepared dishes and steaming vegetables. But I managed very well without it for 30 years and still could. I can't say the same about my pressure cooker.

Modern pressure cookers are safe, practical and easy to use. Not only do they preserve moisture and nutrients, they drastically cut cooking time – a stew may take up to 2 hours to cook in a conventional pot but only 30 minutes in a pressure cooker – and they sterilize preserves in a fraction of the time necessary with the boiling water method.

Food processor and blender

Though not indispensable, both save time and are worth having in the kitchen. I would also add a grinder for dried herbs and spices. An ordinary coffee grinder will do, if used only for this purpose. A mortar and pestle will do the same job as a spice grinder if you're prepared to use lots of elbow grease.

Food mill

Another favorite utensil of mine, the food mill makes fluffy mashed potatoes. It also removes skin and pits from cooked fruits, thus freeing me from the task of peeling and coring apples. It can be replaced with a conical metal sieve and pestle, called a *chinois*.

Canning jars

I am all for recycling but not when it comes to canning jars. Do not use commercial jars that contained mayonnaise, peanut butter or other store-bought food. They may break when heated and the lids will not seal.

Canning jars are available in different sizes, from tiny to jumbo. And some are decorated, which makes them perfect for gifts. Discard any chipped or cracked jar. I use jars with screw-on rings that hold a flat lid with a rubber seal. If using the clamp-type jar, change the rubber ring after each use.

Other useful items

A wide-mouth funnel, clamps to handle hot jars, a jelly bag (I use an old pillowcase) and a timer. A kitchen scale is handy but not essential.

TIPS

Pectin

What makes jams and jellies set? It is the combination of pectin (a gum-like substance contained in fruits), sugar and acid in the right proportions. Some fruits have more pectin than others. Baking apples, citrus fruits, gooseberries, black and red currants, firm plums, quinces and cranberries have a high pectin content. Raspberries, blackberries, soft plums and apricots have a medium pectin content. Strawberries, rhubarb, cherries, peaches, pears, pineapple, melon and grapes are low in pectin. Very ripe fruits have less pectin than less ripe ones.

To increase the pectin content of jam, you have several alternatives :

- Use a commercial pectin. It is available in powder or liquid form. Follow the instructions on the package.
- Use home-made pectin. Crabapple or wild apple juice is the best. Cook apples in a little water until soft. Drain overnight in a jelly bag and use the liquid for pectin.
- Add lemon juice (the juice of one lemon is usually enough) to your jam or jelly.

Never reduce the sugar content of jellies or they may not set.

STIRRING

Don't forget to keep stirring! When cooking sauces, jams and jellies, first you must stir to dissolve the sugar, and then to prevent burning and sticking.

TO SKIM OR NOT TO SKIM

When jams and jellies cook, a light foam forms on the surface. Most of it will disappear during cooking but what's left can be skimmed off with a perforated metal spoon or skimmer. It is essential to skim foam off jellies to get a clear, translucent look but skimming is optional when making jams.

TO WASH OR NOT TO WASH

Vegetables and most fruits need to be washed before being processed. I avoid washing strawberries and raspberries because they soak up water, which increases the cooking time and dilutes their flavor. But my fruits are organically grown and usually clean when picked. I remove any dirt present with a paper towel.

SPRING

Strawberry-Tarragon Jam

Mint-Rhubarb Juice

Rhubarb-Orange Compote

Crêpes

Aumônières

STRAWBERRY-TARRAGON JAM

Siberian by birth, tarragon is French by taste. A mainstay of *cuisine du terroir,* or country cooking, its fragrant taste goes well with eggs, poultry and fish. It flavors vinegars and mustards and can be added fresh to salads. A hardy perennial, tarragon is a worthwhile plant to have in the garden. The leaves freeze well and I always keep a couple of bags handy to add to soups, mashed potatoes or omelettes. Because tarragon reaches its peak at the same time as strawberries, I decided to combine them both in a jam.

INGREDIENTS

5 cups (1.25 L) crushed strawberries
4 cups (1 L) sugar
1/2 cup (125 mL) fresh tarragon leaves, finely chopped

METHOD

1. Put strawberries and sugar in heavy saucepan and bring slowly to a boil, stirring constantly to dissolve sugar.

2. Add tarragon leaves. Reduce heat and simmer, stirring often (to prevent burning) until thickened, about 15 minutes.

3. Ladle into hot sterilized jars and seal.

Makes 3 1/2 cups (875 mL).

This pink, refreshing juice makes wonderful summer drinks. Just plop a few scoops of frozen juice in the blender, add water and whisk at maximum. You can also make popsicles and slush with it.

INGREDIENTS

12 cups (3 L) rhubarb, in chunks
2 cups (500 mL) water
10 sprigs of mint, tied in a bunch
3 cups (750 mL) sugar

METHOD

1. In large pot, bring rhubarb and water to a boil, reduce heat and cook until soft.

2. Drain overnight in jelly bag or a sieve lined with cheesecloth (I use an old pillow case). Discard pulp. Measure juice and add enough water to make 4 cups (1 L).

3. Combine juice, mint sprigs and sugar in a heavy saucepan. Bring slowly to a boil while stirring. Cook for 5 minutes.

4. Remove mint, cool, then pour in rigid containers and freeze.

Makes about 4 cups (1 L).

RHUBARB-ORANGE COMPOTE

This tangy compote can serve many purposes: to fill crêpes and pies, to flavor muffins or to combine with cottage cheese or ricotta to make a refreshing breakfast.

INGREDIENTS

3 oranges
8 cups (2 L) rhubarb, in chunks
4 cups (1 L) sugar
pinch of nutmeg and cinnamon

METHOD

1. Grate orange peel. Then peel orange with sharp knife, removing the white layer. Chop the pulp, removing the seeds as you go.

2. Combine all ingredients in heavy saucepan and bring slowly to a boil, while stirring. Reduce heat and cook until thick (20 to 25 minutes).

3. Ladle into hot, sterilized jars and seal. Or cool and freeze.

Makes 4 cups (1 L).

CRÊPES

When I was a child, February 2 was an important culinary date for me. It was the only day of the year my father made crêpes (very thin pancakes). The occasion was *La Chandeleur* (Candlemas), the celebration of the presentation of the Infant Jesus to the Temple and the purification of the Virgin Mary. Only later did I discover the meaning of this family tradition.

La Chandeleur coincides with the beginning of the planting season. The crêpe, with its golden sheen and circular shape, represents the life-giving sun. It is customary in France to flip the crêpes in the air while holding a gold coin in the palm of your hand. The coin is supposed to bring fortune and success during the year. Woe betide the cook who drops a pancake!

It is said that Napoleon made crêpes shortly before leaving for the Russian front. He successfully flipped four but dropped the fifth. This worried him greatly. He did win four great victories. But on the day Moscow burned, the Emperor turned to Marechal Ney, his second in command, and said "It is the fifth crêpe."

To make perfect crêpes, let the batter stand for at least 2 hours before cooking. Use a very hot skillet, preferably cast iron.

INGREDIENTS

1 1/2 cups (375 mL) flour	2 tbsp (30 mL) sugar
3 eggs	1 tbsp (15 mL) oil
2 cups (500 mL) milk	1/2 cup (125 mL) water (if needed)
1 tbsp (15 mL) vanilla extract	pinch of salt

METHOD

1. Beat together 1/2 cup (125 mL) milk with eggs, oil, vanilla and sugar. Stir in flour alternating with remaining milk until smooth. Let stand in cool place for 2 hours. The batter should coat the back of a spoon with a thin film. If too thick, stir in a little water.

2. Cook thin crêpes in a hot, lightly greased skillet. When the surface starts to bubble they are ready to flip.

3. Eat right away or cool and freeze any extras. Wrap crêpes in packages of 6 or 10 in plastic film and place in a plastic bag and seal. They will keep in the freezer for a couple of months.

Makes 24 to 28 crêpes.

AUMÔNIÈRES

Aumônières were small purses tied with a string and usually worn hanging from a belt.

INGREDIENTS

1 orange
4 crêpes (see page 26)
1 cup (250 mL) rhubarb-orange compote (see page 25)

METHOD

1. Peel the orange skin in a very thin ribbon, removing as little of the white part as possible. Cut peel lengthwise to make 4 strips. Poach 1 minute in simmering water, drain and cool.

2. Spread crêpes on a working surface. Divide filling among crêpes. Bring sides together to form little bundles and tie with orange strips.

3. Finish peeling the orange, this time removing all white part. Cut 4 slices crosswise, each 1/2 inch (1 cm) wide. Remove pits and arrange slices on a baking dish.

4. Place a crêpe bundle on each orange slice. Crush remaining orange and pour juice in the pan. Bake at 375°F (190°C), 5 to 10 minutes.

5. Serve warm over strawberry coulis or custard.

Makes 4 portions.

Variation: Substitute plum marmalade with rum (see page 109) for the rhubarb-orange compote.

S U M M E R

Raspberry Syrup
Raspberry and Mango Jam
Gooseberry-Lemon Verbena Jelly
Almond-Peach Jam
Angostura-Peach Jam
Peach Halves in Syrup
Apricot Halves in Liqueur
Apricot and Honey Compote
Peach Melba
Apricot Tartlets
Antipasto
Curried Sliced Pickles
Eggplant in Oil
Pickled Beets with Star Anise
Dill Pickles
Mustard Pickle Slices
Herb-Flavored Oil
Pizza Oil
Herb Vinegar
Pizza Herb Mix
Herbed Yogurt Cheese
Herb Mix for Seafood
Salmon Ceviche
Herb Salt for Seafood
Herb Salt for Poultry
Cajun Spices
Venison Spice Mix
No-Cholesterol Baked Beans
La Bomba
Harissa
Curry Powder
Clarified Butter
Lamb Curry
Oven-Dried Tomatoes
Pistou and Pesto

RASPBERRY SYRUP

I use the following method to make all kinds of fruit syrups: blackberry, blueberry, gooseberry, red currant, grape or any other fruit. Delicious on pancakes, over ice cream or in cool drinks, syrups also make colorful and tasty popsicles.

INGREDIENTS

raspberries
water
sugar

METHOD

1. Place fruit in large pot. Add enough water to cover 1 inch (2.5 cm) of the bottom of the pot. Bring slowly to a boil while crushing the fruit. Cook for 1 minute.

2. Drain overnight in jelly bag or a sieve lined with cheesecloth. Discard pulp.

3. Put juice in heavy saucepan. Add sugar to taste. The more sugar you add, the longer the syrup will keep.

4. Dissolve sugar over low heat, while stirring. To keep the flavor of fresh fruit, do not boil or overcook.

5. Pour syrup into clean bottles. Seal and keep in the refrigerator up to a month. Or freeze.

RASPBERRY AND MANGO JAM

Mangoes are available all year, but can be found at bargain prices in early summer, just when my raspberry canes are heavy with fruit. I got the idea of this jam by making a fruit salad. The marriage of raspberries and mango was so perfect, it was meant to be preserved.

INGREDIENTS

3 mangoes, about 2 lb (1 kg)
1 1/2 cups (375 mL) raspberries
1 cup (250 mL) sugar

METHOD

1. Peel mangoes, remove pits and purée flesh in blender or food processor.

2. Combine mango pulp, raspberries and sugar in heavy saucepan. Bring slowly to a boil, while stirring. Reduce heat and cook until thick, about 15 minutes.

3. Ladle into jars, seal and keep in the refrigerator up to 4 months. Or freeze.

Makes about 2 1/3 cups (600 mL).

Variation: When I have raspberries galore, I remove the tiny seeds by pressing the crushed raspberries through a fine sieve and reduce the cooking time to make a smooth and creamy compote.

GOOSEBERRY-LEMON VERBENA JELLY

Lemon verbena is a deciduous bush that can reach 13 feet (4 m) and more in its native Chile. In northern climates, this graceful plant should be grown in a greenhouse or in a pot and brought inside during the winter, as it is very sensitive to frost. The pointed thin leaves are pale green and give off a wonderful lemony scent. They can be used fresh, dried or frozen to make a digestive tea. Tiny mauve flowers appear midsummer and make lovely decoration for cakes.

INGREDIENTS

3 cups (750 mL) gooseberry (or red currant) juice
1 cup (250 mL) packed fresh lemon verbena leaves
3 cups (750 mL) sugar

METHOD

1. Place fruit in large pot. Add enough water to cover 1 inch (2.5 cm) of the bottom of the pot. Bring slowly to a boil while crushing the fruit. Cook for 1 minute.

2. Drain overnight in jelly bag or a sieve lined with cheesecloth. Discard pulp.

3. Put juice in heavy saucepan. Add sugar to taste. The more sugar you add, the longer the syrup will keep.

4. Dissolve sugar over low heat, while stirring. To keep the flavor of fresh fruit, do not boil or overcook.

5. Tie lemon verbena leaves in cheesecloth. Put all ingredients in a heavy pot. Bring slowly to a boil, while stirring. Cook until jelly point, 10 to 12 minutes.

6. Remove verbena leaves. Ladle jelly into jars and seal.

Makes 4 cups (1 L).

ALMOND-PEACH JAM

Greek mythology relates the story of Phyllis who was made so unhappy by the desertion of her husband Demophon that she died of grief. Touched by her tragic demise, the gods changed her into an almond tree. When Demophon returned and was shown the leafless and forlorn tree, he embraced it and it burst into bloom. And thus the almond tree became the emblem of true love.

INGREDIENTS

6 peaches, in chunks, about 4 cups (1L)
1 cup (250 mL) sugar
1 tbsp (15 mL) almond extract

METHOD

1. Put all ingredients in heavy saucepan. Bring slowly to a boil, while stirring. Reduce heat and simmer until thick, about 10 minutes.

2. Ladle into jars and seal. Keeps 3 months in the refrigerator.

Makes 3 cups (750 mL).

ANGOSTURA-PEACH JAM

Angostura is a bitter made with the bark of Cusparia, a South American bush with tonic and fever reducing properties. The pungent liquid was created in Angostura (today Ciudad Bolívar), Venezuela, by an army surgeon to alleviate the effects of the tropical climate.

Only a few drops enhance drinks and flavor salads, soups and sauces. Angostura seems to go naturally with most pitted fruits like peaches and cherries.

INGREDIENTS

6 peaches, in chunks, about 4 cups (1 L)
1 cup (250 mL) sugar
10 drops Angostura

METHOD

1. Put all ingredients in heavy saucepan. Bring slowly to a boil, while stirring. Reduce heat and simmer until thick, about 10 minutes.

2. Ladle into jars and seal. Keeps 3 months in the refrigerator.

Makes 3 cups (750 mL).

PEACH HALVES IN SYRUP

The peach was very popular at the court of Louis XIV, where it was called *tétons de Vénus* or Venus' breasts, I suppose in reference to its soft, silky skin, voluptuous curves and rosy complexion.

Ingredients

sugar
water
peaches

Method

1. Prepare a medium-thick syrup by dissolving 1 cup (250 mL) sugar and 2 cups (500 mL) water. This will fill 2 jars. Multiply the amount by the number of jars you wish to make. Bring to a boil, then cool.

2. Peel peaches. Cut in half and remove pits.

3. Arrange peach halves in clean jars and cover with syrup, leaving ¾ inch (2 cm) head space. Seal and process for 20 minutes in boiling water or 5 minutes in pressure cooker.

Variation: Add a few teaspoons of liqueur or fruit alcohol to each jar.

Tip: To peel peaches (or tomatoes), plunge in boiling water for 1 to 2 minutes then immediately place them in ice-cold water. The skin should slide off easily.

APRICOT HALVES IN LIQUEUR

The apricot tree was first believed to have come from ancient Armenia, thus its Latin name, *Prunus armeniaca.* It was later discovered that it grew in China well before its introduction into Persian gardens.

INGREDIENTS

3 cups (750 mL) sugar
2 1/2 cups (625 mL) water
6 1/2 pounds (3 kg) apricots, ripe but still firm
1/2 cup (125 mL) Southern Comfort or other orange liqueur

METHOD

1. Dissolve sugar in water over medium heat.

2. Cut apricots in half, remove pits and add to the syrup. Bring to a boil, then remove from heat.

3. Divide alcohol among jars, fill with apricot halves and cover with warm syrup, leaving 3/4 inch (2 cm) head space.

4. Eliminate bubbles by tapping jars delicately on the counter and seal.

Makes 8 cups (2 L).

APRICOT AND HONEY COMPOTE

In the mid-16th century, northern Europe suffered a honey shortage, not because bees went on strike, but as a result of the breakup of monasteries by the Reformation. At that time, monks raised bees as a source of wax for votive candles and consequently were the main producers of honey.

Smooth and fragrant, this compote goes well with yogurt and ricotta cheese for breakfast or dessert.

INGREDIENTS

2 cups (500 mL) puréed apricots
1 cup (250 mL) liquid honey

METHOD

1. Combine ingredients in heavy saucepan and bring slowly to a boil. Reduce heat and simmer until thick.

2. Ladle into jars and seal. Keeps 3 months in the refrigerator.

Makes 2 cups (500 mL).

PEACH MELBA

Nellie Melba was a famous Australian singer. When she visited London in 1894 to sing at Covent Garden, the celebrated chef Auguste Escoffier created this sinful dessert, now a staple of French ice-cream parlors.

Ingredients

gooseberry-lemon verbena jelly (see page 36)
vanilla ice cream
peach halves in syrup

Method

1. Melt jelly in a little water over low heat or in microwave. Cool.

2. Fill tall glasses with 2 scoops of vanilla ice cream, garnish with 2 peach halves and pour jelly over. Top with whipped cream, if desired.

APRICOT TARTLETS

By using prepared shells, this light dessert is ready in 5 minutes.

INGREDIENTS

6 tartlet shells
1 cup (250 mL) ricotta cheese
1 cup (250 mL) apricot and honey compote (see page 45)
1 jar apricot halves in liqueur (see page 44)

METHOD

1. Cook shells and cool.

2. Combine ricotta cheese with apricot and honey compote.

3. Fill shells with mixture and top each with one apricot half. Serve cool.

Makes 6 tartlets.

ANTIPASTO

Arranging vegetables to make pretty patterns may be pleasing to the eye, but it is also a time-consuming, sometimes frustrating task that requires too much food handling for my taste. I am content with a more casual look.

INGREDIENTS

2 cups (500 mL) cauliflower chunks	8 cups (2 L) water
1 cup (250 mL) broccoli chunks	2 cups (500 mL) white vinegar
2 zucchini cut in sticks	1/4 cup (60 mL) sugar
2 carrots cut in sticks	5 garlic cloves
2 celery branches cut diagonally in chunks	5 dried or 2 fresh chili peppers,
2 kohlrabi cut in sticks	chopped
20 pearl onions	2 tsp (5 mL) mustard seeds
1 cup (250 mL) pickling salt	1 tbsp (15 mL) cloves

METHOD

1. In large bowl, arrange vegetables in layers, sprinkling salt between each layer.

2. Add 6 cups (1.5 L) of water. Cover bowl with plastic film and place a weight on top to prevent the vegetables from floating. Keep in the refrigerator overnight.

3. Drain, rinse under cold water for 2 minutes and drain again.

4. Combine 2 cups (500 mL) water with vinegar and sugar. Dissolve sugar over low heat.

5. Divide garlic, chili peppers and spices among the jars. Pack with vegetables. Cover with sugared vinegar, leaving 1 1/4 inches (3 cm) head space.

6. Seal and process 20 minutes in boiling water or 5 minutes in pressure cooker. Wait 3 weeks before tasting.

Makes 10 cups (2.5 L).

CURRIED SLICED PICKLES

For thousands of years, mustard seeds were crushed and mixed with vinegar to make a condiment. The Romans replaced the vinegar with unfermented grape juice or "must." *Mustum ardens* or "hot must" gave us the word "mustard."

INGREDIENTS

3 pounds (1.5 kg) medium pickling cucumbers
1 tsp (5 mL) curry powder (see page 81)
2 cups (500 mL) cider vinegar
2 1/2 cups (625 mL) sugar
1 tbsp (15 mL) mustard seeds
1 tbsp (15 mL) celery seeds

Brine
1/2 cup (125 mL) pickling salt, dissolved in
8 cups (2 L) water

METHOD

1. Wash cucumbers and cut in slices 1/4 inch (5 mm) thick. Cover with brine and let stand for 5 hours.

2. Rinse under cold water and drain.

3. Combine remaining ingredients and bring to a boil. Add cucumber slices. Bring back to a boil, then remove from heat.

4. Pack slices into hot, sterilized jars, cover with cooking liquid and seal.

Makes 8 cups (2 L).

EGGPLANT IN OIL

Because it is related to the mandrake, which was used in witchcraft in medieval times, the eggplant was once believed to provoke insanity. Sixteenth century botanists called it "fool's apple." Widely used in Mediterranean and Oriental cooking, it is particularly popular in Japan.

This salad in a jar is fabulous on its own as an appetizer, served over thinly shredded cabbage for a light lunch or puréed as a creamy dip.

INGREDIENTS

2 pounds (1 kg) eggplant
salt
1 chili pepper, fresh or dried
2 garlic cloves
2 tbsp (30 mL) cider vinegar
2 sprigs rosemary
2 sprigs thyme
salt and pepper
olive oil

METHOD

1. Pick small eggplants, firm to the touch. Cut in cubes and sprinkle with salt. Let stand a couple of hours. Rinse briefly under cold water.

2. Bring large pot of water to a boil and blanch eggplants for 2 minutes. Drain and press with a spoon to extract all the water.

3. Remove seeds from chili pepper and mince. In mortar, crush garlic with pepper, adding the vinegar a little at a time. Add minced herbs, salt and pepper. If you don't have mortar, chop garlic finely or crush with garlic press, and then mix with herbs and add vinegar.

4. Fill jars with eggplants and herb mix without pressing. Cover with olive oil. Seal and place in the sun. Shake jars or mix the contents delicately with a spoon every day for two weeks. Then enjoy!

Makes 6 cups (1.5 L).

PICKLED BEETS WITH STAR ANISE

Star anise! Well, you just have to look at this pretty, sweet-smelling spice to know where the name comes from. It is the fruit of the badiana tree, originally from China. In Japan the tree is planted in temple gardens and on tombs. The powdered bark is used as incense.

Both a stimulant and a diuretic, with carminative properties as well, star anise will promote digestion and sweeten the breath if chewed in small quantities after a meal.

INGREDIENTS

6 pounds (2.75 kg) small beets (50 to 60)
2 cups (500 mL) cider vinegar
2 cups (500 mL) water
2 cups (500 mL) sugar
4 star anise
1 tsp (5 mL) fennel seeds
1 tsp (5 mL) cloves
1 tsp (5 mL) peppercorns

METHOD

1. Cut off beet leaves, leaving ¾ inch (2 cm) stems at crown. Cook beets until tender. Cool and peel.

2. Combine vinegar, water, sugar and spices in heavy pot. Bring to a boil, add beets, then reduce heat and simmer 10 minutes.

3. Pack beets into hot, sterilized jars. Fill with cooking liquid and seal.

Makes 14 cups (3.5 L) or 7 16-ounce (500 mL) jars.

"Gather the tops of the ripest dill and cover the bottom of the vessel, and lay a layer of cucumbers and another of dill till you have filled the vessel within a handful of the top. Then take as much water as you think will fill the vessel and mix it with salt and a quarter of a pound of allom to a gallon of water and pour it on them and press them down with a stone on them and keep them covered close. For that use I think the water will be best boy'ld and cold, which will keep longer sweet, or if you like not this pickle, doe it with water, salt and white wine vinegar, or (if you please) pour the water and salt on them scalding hot which will make them ready to use the sooner." (from *Receipt Book* by Joseph Cooper, cook to Charles I, 1640).

Ingredients

25 pickling cucumbers 2 to 3 inches long (5 to 7 cm)
4 cups (1 L) cider vinegar
1 1/2 cups (375 mL) sugar
2 tbsp (30 mL) mustard seeds
2 tbsp (30 mL) celery or fennel seeds
4 sprigs fresh dill

Brine
1 cup (250 mL) pickling salt, dissolved in
8 cups (2 L) water

Method

1. Wash cucumbers. Soak 24 hours in brine. Drain and pat dry.

2. Bring vinegar, sugar and spices to a boil. Add cucumbers and cook 5 minutes over medium heat.

3. Pack cucumbers and spices in hot, sterilized jars. Cover with cooking liquid and seal. Wait a month before opening.

Makes 8 cups (2L).

MUSTARD PICKLE SLICES

In India, turmeric plays a role in wedding ceremonies. The groom wraps a thread covered with turmeric paste around the bride's neck. In Malaysia, turmeric paste is spread on the umbilical cord of newborn babies and on the mother's belly as an antiseptic and to chase away evil spirits.

Ingredients

10 medium pickling cucumbers
1 cup (250 mL) white vinegar
1 cup (250 mL) water
1 cup (250 mL) brown sugar
1 tsp (5 mL) powdered mustard
1 tsp (5 mL) turmeric
¼ tsp (1 mL) allspice
¼ tsp (1 mL) powdered cumin

Brine
¼ cup (60 mL) salt, dissolved in
2 cups (500 mL) water

Method

1. Wash cucumbers and cut into slices ¼ inch (5 mm) thick. Cover with brine and let stand for 5 hours.

2. Rinse under cold water and drain.

3. Combine remaining ingredients and bring to a boil. Add cucumber slices. Bring back to a boil, then remove from heat.

4. Pack slices into hot, sterilized jars, cover with cooking liquid and seal.

Makes 3 16-ounce (500 mL) jars.

HERB-FLAVORED OIL

Native to the eastern Mediterranean, the olive tree can live thousands of years. So it is quite possible that the olive trees now standing at Gethsemane garden were there when Jesus prayed in the garden, nearly 2000 years ago.

Ingredients

2 garlic cloves, crushed
2 sprigs fresh rosemary
10 sprigs fresh marjoram
6 peppercorns
1 pinch fennel seeds
1 sprig fresh dill or summer savory
2 cups (500 mL) olive oil

Method

Place herbs and spices in clean bottle and fill with oil. Seal and let the flavors blend for a week before using.

Makes 2 cups (500 mL).

PIZZA OIL

"Olive oil is the very soul of a salad, and far beyond this, for it is one of the finest foods and medicines ever bestowed upon man.... A teaspoon a day, taken with vegetables in the course of the daily meals, will calm the troubles of many a storm-tossed digestion, and make the world a better place for the brief dwelling of man."
(*The Epicure's Companion*, E. Buyard, 1937).

INGREDIENTS

2 garlic cloves
1 or 2 chili peppers
1 sprig fresh rosemary
4 peppercorns
1 cup (250 mL) olive oil

METHOD

Place herbs and spices in clean bottle and fill with oil. Seal and let the flavours blend for a week before using.

Makes 2 cups (500 mL).

HERB VINEGAR

Digestive, stimulant and disinfectant, apple cider vinegar has been used for cooking and medicine since ancient times. Hippocrates prescribed it for various ailments. More recently, cider vinegar has been used to treat arthritis, obesity, high blood pressure and migraines.

Always choose a pure, natural apple cider vinegar.

INGREDIENTS

1 sprig fresh rosemary
5 sprigs fresh marjoram or oregano
4 sage leaves

1 garlic clove, crushed
4 cups (1 L) apple cider vinegar

METHOD

Combine all ingredients in bottle. Seal and keep one month before using in salad dressing or sauces.

Makes 4 cups (1 L).

PIZZA HERB MIX

Use dried herbs to make this mix and keep it close at hand. You'll want to use it on everything, not only on pizza.

INGREDIENTS

1/3 cup (75 mL) rosemary
1/3 cup (75 mL) basil

2 tbsp (30 mL) summer savory
2 tbsp (30 mL) marjoram

METHOD

Grind or crush herbs, mix well and store in sealed glass jar.

Makes 1/2 cup (125 mL).

HERBED YOGURT CHEESE

This cheese is light (especially if you use low-fat yogurt) and easy to digest. To get the right consistency, use only natural yogurt made without gelatin or other thickeners.

INGREDIENTS

4 cups (1 L) plain yogurt
2 tbsp (30 mL) pizza herb mix (see page 65)
1 tsp (5 mL) salt

METHOD

1. To make yogurt cheese, place yogurt into jelly bag or sieve lined with cheesecloth. Drain overnight in the refrigerator.

2. Combine cheese with herb mix and salt. Serve as an appetizer or a spread.

Makes 3 cups (750 mL).

HERB MIX FOR SEAFOOD

In medieval times, bouquets of fennel were hung over doorways to ward off evil spells. Fennel was also stuffed in keyholes on the Sabbath to prevent witches from entering the house.

Rub fish with this mix before grilling.

INGREDIENTS

peel of 2 lemons
2 tbsp (30 mL) dill or fennel seeds
1/3 cup (75 mL) dried dill, crushed

METHOD

1. Peel lemons as thinly as possible. Dry peel in the sun (it may take several days) or in the oven, 20 minutes at the lowest temperature.

2. Crush or grind peel and seeds. Combine with dill and keep in sealed jar.

Makes about 1/2 cup (125 mL).

SALMON CEVICHE

It is essential that the salmon be extra fresh. You may also use trout fillets.

INGREDIENTS

1 salmon fillet, about 14 ounces (400 g)
2 tbsp (30 mL) herb mix for seafood (see page 69)
peel and juice of 2 limes
1 French baguette
olive oil
1 green onion, minced
salt
fresh dill

METHOD

1. Cut salmon in thin strips and arrange on a shallow dish. Sprinkle with herb mix and minced or grated lime peel, and cover with lime juice. Cover dish with plastic film and let stand overnight in the refrigerator.

2. Cut baguette in half lengthwise, then in 2-inch (5 cm) strips. Brush with olive oil and broil until golden.

3. Sprinkle minced onion over bread, top with salmon and decorate with fresh dill. Serve chilled.

Makes 4 portions as appetizer.

HERB SALT FOR SEAFOOD

There are two ways of grinding herbs and spices. The fast and easy way is to use a spice grinder or a coffee grinder used specifically for this purpose. The fun way is to crush them with a mortar and pestle, preferably large and made of stone or porcelain. This "ancient" way may require more elbow grease but it is agreeably silent and gives you a noseful of aromatic fragrances.

INGREDIENTS

1 tbsp (15 mL) fennel or dill seeds
1 tbsp (15 mL) dried basil
¼ cup (60 mL) dried dill
1 pinch cumin
⅔ cup (150 mL) sea salt

METHOD

Grind or crush seeds. Combine with remaining ingredients. Keep in sealed jar.

Makes about 1 cup (250 mL).

HERB SALT FOR POULTRY

Lovage, unfamiliar to many people, is a versatile and decorative herb. Grown in the garden, the plant can become a green giant of 5 feet. The leaves have a sharp celery-parsley taste. Dried or frozen, they retain their full aroma and are a useful addition to soups, sauces, stews and herb mixes.

INGREDIENTS

1/3 cup (75 mL) dried summer savory
1/3 cup (75 mL) dried rosemary
2 tbsp (30 mL) dried basil
1 tbsp (30 mL) dried lovage
2/3 cup (150 mL) sea salt

METHOD

Combine all ingredients and keep in sealed jar.

Makes about 1 cup (250 mL).

CAJUN SPICES

When my craving for hot and fiery barbecues peaks in early summer, I make this spice mix using up my leftover herbs and peppers from the previous year. Use this mix for "blackened" grilling and other Cajun specialties.

INGREDIENTS

1 tsp (5 mL) cayenne pepper or
   2 small dried, seeded chili peppers
1 tbsp (15 mL) paprika
1 tbsp (15 mL) dried oregano

1 tbsp (15 mL) dried thyme
1 tsp (5 mL) salt
1 tsp (5 mL) dried garlic
1 tsp (5 mL) black peppercorns

METHOD

Combine all ingredients and grind. Keep in a sealed glass jar.

Makes about 1/2 cup (125 mL).

VENISON SPICE MIX

In medieval times, spices such as cinnamon, cloves, cardamom and ginger were used extensively in sauces and marinades for venison, primarily to mask the taste of gamy meat. In this mix, I have tried to capture the essence, but not the pungency, of those early mixes.

   Use in wine-based marinades and no-cholesterol baked beans (see page 77).

INGREDIENTS

1 tbsp (15 mL) black peppercorns
1 tbsp (15 mL) powdered mustard
1 chili pepper, dried
1 tbsp (15 mL) allspice
1 tbsp (15 mL) dill seed

1 tbsp (15 mL) coriander seeds
1 tsp (5 mL) cinnamon
1 tsp (5 mL) powdered clove
1 bay leaf, crushed

METHOD

Combine all ingredients and place in sealed jar. It will keep for up to a year.

Makes about 1/3 cup (75 mL).

NO-CHOLESTEROL BAKED BEANS

Beans are usually cooked with meat to make rich and creamy dishes – cassoulet in France, *fèves au lard* in Québec – loaded with cholesterol. Here is a light version, just as tasty but less deadly.

INGREDIENTS

1 cup (250 mL) dried navy beans
3 medium onions, minced
cooking oil
4 parsnips, peeled and cut in chunks
1 tbsp (15 mL) venison spice mix (see page 76)
2 cups (500 mL) water
salt and pepper

METHOD

1. To reduce flatulence and increase their nutritional value, soak beans in water for up to 3 days until they germinate, changing the water twice a day. If you are in a hurry, soak them 4 to 6 hours.

2. Cook onions in oil until soft.

3. Add parsnips, beans, spices and water. Bring to a boil, then reduce heat and simmer until beans are tender (about 2 hours). The cooking time is reduced to 45 minutes with a pressure cooker.

4. Season to taste.

Makes 4 portions.

LA BOMBA

When making this fiery condiment, do not throw away the seeds of the chili peppers. Dry and grind to powder to spice up dishes. Or keep them in olive oil and use the oil for pizza and Latin dishes.

Ingredients

4 1/2 pounds (2 kg) red bell peppers
1 cup (250 mL) chili peppers
1/2 cup (125 mL) pickling salt
2 garlic heads
1 cup (250 mL) or more olive oil

Method

1. Remove seeds from peppers and chop. In colander, place layers of peppers alternating with pickling salt. Press with a weight and drain overnight.

2. Rinse peppers under cold running water and drain.

3. Peel and mince garlic or crush with a garlic press. Cook garlic in 1/2 cup (125 mL) of olive oil for 3 to 4 minutes.

4. Add peppers. Cook over moderate heat, stirring and adding oil a little at a time until creamy and almost caramelized, about 1 hour.

5. You may ladle the bomba into hot, sterilized jars at this stage or put the mixture through a vegetable masher (food mill) to remove the skin for a creamier texture.

6. Keep mixture in sealed glass jar in refrigerator or freeze. Will keep up to 1 year.

Makes 1 cup (250 mL).

HARISSA

An essential ingredient of couscous, harissa is a north African condiment that will add fire to your Tex-Mex dishes.

Ingredients

10 hot peppers, fresh or dried
3 garlic cloves
1 tsp (5 mL) salt
2 tsp (10 mL) coriander seeds
1 tsp (5 mL) cumin
1 tsp (5 mL) caraway seeds
1 tsp (5 mL) fresh or dried mint
1 cup (250 mL) olive oil

Method

1. Remove seeds from peppers and chop. If dried, soak in water for 20 minutes.

2. Place peppers, garlic and spices in blender or food processor. With machine running, add oil in a slow, steady stream until smooth and creamy.

3. Pour harissa in glass or stone crock, cover with oil and store in refrigerator for up to 6 weeks. Or freeze.

Makes 1 cup (250 mL).

Tip: Use rubber gloves to seed and chop hot peppers.

CURRY POWDER

The name "fenugreek" comes from *Foenum-graecum*, which means Greek hay. In ancient times, the plant was used to scent inferior hay. Today it is still used to flavor cattle food and make damaged hay palatable.

INGREDIENTS

3 cardamom pods
1 tbsp (15 mL) black peppercorns
1 tbsp (15 mL) cumin seeds
1 tbsp (15 mL) caraway seeds
1 small dried hot pepper

1 tsp (5 mL) turmeric
1 tsp (5 mL) mustard seeds
1 tsp (5 mL) cinnamon
1 tsp (5 mL) fenugreek

METHOD

Combine ingredients and grind to powder in blender or spice grinder. Store in sealed glass jar. After a couple of months, the flavors will begin to dissipate and it's time to make a fresh batch.

CLARIFIED BUTTER

Also know as ghee, clarified butter has a much higher smoking temperature than regular butter, making it perfect for sautéing meat at high temperatures. It is also delicious with seafood, like steamed lobster or crab.

METHOD

Melt butter over low heat or in microwave. Allow to stand a few minutes. Skim foam off top and carefully pour the liquid into a container, leaving the solids behind.

LAMB CURRY

Curry comes from *kari*, a Tamil word meaning sauce. The name refers to the mix of spices as well as any dish flavored with it.

Ingredients

2 pounds (1 kg) lamb in cubes
2 cups (500 mL) plain yogurt
1/4 cup (60 mL) clarified butter (see page 81)
1 large onion, minced
4 garlic cloves, minced
1 tbsp (15 mL) minced fresh ginger
4 tbsp (60 mL) curry powder (see page 81)
salt and pepper
1 cup (250 mL) water
fresh mint or coriander

Method

1. Marinate lamb in yogurt for 1 hour at room temperature or overnight in the refrigerator. Drain, reserving the marinade, and pat dry.

2. Cook onion, garlic and ginger in clarified butter for 1 minute. Sprinkle with curry powder and cook 30 seconds. Add lamb and stir to coat it well with spices. Add water and season to taste.

3. Cover and simmer 1 hour or until lamb is tender. Gradually add more water if necessary.

4. Add yogurt marinade just before serving. Heat through without boiling. Serve sprinkled with mint or coriander.

Makes 4 portions.

OVEN-DRIED TOMATOES

You may use any variety of tomatoes for drying, except cherry tomatoes. To reduce the drying time, choose firm fleshy fruits with few seeds. I have tried plum (Italian) tomatoes and regular tomatoes and found little difference in the weight or quality of the finished product.

Dried tomatoes are sometimes preserved in oil, but I prefer to keep them dry. This means less mess when the time comes to use them.

Method

1. Cut tomatoes in quarters or in half if small. Place on baking sheet and dry in the oven at the lowest temperature (150°F or 65°C) for 18 to 24 hours, until leathery.

2. Store in glass jar.

3. Rehydrate in warm water for 20 minutes before using in sauces, salads and various other dishes.

Variation: You can sprinkle herbs (try the pizza herb mix on page 65) on the tomatoes before drying.

PISTOU AND PESTO

Both names come from the Italian *pestare*, meaning to crush, and both are made with fresh basil leaves, garlic, olive oil, grated Parmesan cheese and, in the case of the Italian pesto, pine nuts. In Provence, *pistou* also refers to a hearty vegetable and noodle soup, to which the garlic paste is added before serving. Quantities of each ingredient will depend on your supply of basil and your garlic threshold.

INGREDIENTS

basil leaves
garlic
olive oil
grated Parmesan cheese
pine nuts, optional

METHOD

1. Place basil and garlic in blender or food processor. Process to a smooth paste, adding oil in a stream.

2. Add cheese and, if making pesto, pine nuts and process a few more seconds, leaving the nuts in small chunks to add texture.

Tip for freezing: When preparing pesto for freezing, omit the garlic as it acquires a stronger taste when frozen, and omit the cheese, which tends to clump up when defrosted. Add both ingredients before serving.

FALL

PEARS IN WINE

It took dedication and time for ancient botanists to create the pear tree as we know it today. The wild variety produced fruit no bigger than a pea.

INGREDIENTS

2 cups (500 mL) water or grape juice
2 cups (500 mL) red wine
1 cup (250 mL) sugar
4 cloves
1 star anise
1 stick cinnamon or 1 tsp (15 mL) powder
1 tsp (15 mL) ground coriander
8 to 10 pears

METHOD

1. Combine water, wine, sugar and spices. Dissolve sugar over low heat. Cool, then strain to remove spices.

2. Cut pears in half. Peel and core. Pack in jars without bruising the fruit. Cover with syrup. Seal and process, 10 minutes in a pressure cooker or 30 minutes in boiling water.

Makes 4 16-ounce (500 mL) jars.

PEAR MILLE-FEUILLE

Mille-feuille means "thousand layers" and is made with puff pastry. I once attempted to make puff pastry and quickly concluded it was a task best left to professionals. Thankfully, the commercial dough gives excellent results.

Ingredients

1 package puff pastry
1 jar pears in wine (see page 91)
1 cup (250 mL) heavy cream
1 tbsp (15 mL) sugar
icing sugar (optional)

Method

1. A commercial package of puff pastry usually contains 2 blocks. Roll out each in a rectangle 12 inches by 4 inches (30 x 10 cm), and cut in thirds.

2. Place dough on baking sheet and bake 20 minutes at 350°F (180°C) until puffed and flaky. Cool.

3. Drain pears and set aside. Reduce pear juice over low heat until thick. Cool. (You can do this in advance.)

4. Just before serving, whip cream and sugar.

5. Cut pears in slices. Cut mille-feuilles in half, lengthwise. Spread some whipped cream on the bottom half. Arrange pears on top and cover with more cream. Top with the other half of pastry. Sprinkle with icing sugar, if desired.

6. Divide the syrup among the serving plates. Place mille-feuilles on top and serve.

Makes 6 portions.

Tip: When making whipped cream, chill the bowl and beaters in the freezer for 10 minutes first. The cream will hold better. And do not overbeat or it will turn into butter.

FRENCH PEAR TART

Vanilla is the fruit of an orchid vine. Because the flower cannot self-pollinate, it needs the help of a bee – or a human – to bear fruit. A skilled person can pollinate up to 2000 flowers a day.

INGREDIENTS

1 pie shell
1 tbsp (15 mL) cornstarch
1/2 cup (125 mL) cup milk
2 tbsp (30 mL) sugar
1 tsp (5 mL) vanilla extract
1 jar pears in pineapple juice (see page 96)
2 eggs

METHOD

1. Bake pie shell 10 minutes at 375°F (190°C).

2. Dissolve corn starch in a little milk. Heat remaining milk with sugar and vanilla.

3. Drain pears and arrange in pie shell.

4. Beat eggs into cornstarch mixture and add warm milk. Pour over pears. Bake 30 minutes or until firm to the touch.

5. You can sprinkle sugar over the top and broil a few minutes until caramelized. Serve warm or cold.

Makes 4 to 6 portions.

PEAR AND PINEAPPLE COMPOTE

Because the fruit resembles a pine cone, the British named it "pine-apple." But in Central America they call it *nana-nana*, meaning "perfume of perfumes."

INGREDIENTS

2 pineapples, 3 pounds (1.5 kg) each
4 pears
4 cups (1 L) sugar

METHOD

1. Peel pineapple and remove woody center. Peel and core pears.

2. Purée fruits in food processor or blender. The texture can be smooth or crunchy, according to your taste.

3. Combine fruit purée and sugar. Cook over medium heat, while stirring until thick, about 30 minutes. Thickness is also a question of taste. I like my compote smooth and thick.

4. Ladle into hot, sterilized jars and seal. Keep in the refrigerator up to 3 months or freeze.

Makes 8 cups (2 L).

PEARS IN PINEAPPLE JUICE

These pears are excellent for babies...and for grown-ups too!

INGREDIENTS

pears
pure pineapple juice

METHOD

1. Cut pears in half. Peel and core. Pack 3 medium pears in each 16-ounce (500 mL) jar. Cover with pineapple juice.

2. Seal and process 30 minutes in boiling water or 10 minutes in a pressure cooker.

APPLE-LEMON MARMALADE

"In our garden, an old secular priest looked after a number of lemon trees....
When the lemons were ripe, they were picked with care, wrapped singly in
soft paper, packed and sent off.... Such an orangery was regarded by middle
class families as a capital investment which would pay a certain interest every
year." (*Italian Journey* 1786–88, Goethe)

INGREDIENTS

4 lemons
3 cups (750 mL) water
3 pounds (1.5 kg) cooking apples (about 12 medium)
6 cups (1.5 L) sugar
6 mint sprigs, tied up in cheesecloth

METHOD

1. Cut lemons in two and slice thinly, removing pits. Soak in water
   overnight. Cook over moderate heat until peel is tender, about 10 minutes.

2. Peel and core apples. Cut in thin slices. Combine apples, lemons with their
   liquid, sugar and mint.

3. Bring to a boil while stirring. Reduce heat and cook until thick, about
   30 minutes.

4. Remove mint. Ladle into hot, sterilized jars and seal.

Makes 4 16-ounce (500 mL) jars.

*Variation: Prepare orange ratafia (see page 159) at the same time as this
marmalade and replace the lemons in this recipe with the leftover juice and pulp.
Skip the soaking step.*

CRABAPPLE-ROSEMARY JELLY

I use this fragrant jelly to make a sauce for liver or lamb chops. Combine 1 tbsp (15 mL) jelly, 1 tbsp (15 mL) balsamic vinegar and 1 tbsp (15 mL) white vermouth or water. Heat a few seconds in the microwave oven or in a pan to dissolve the jelly. Cook meat and set aside. Deglaze frying pan with the sauce, reduce over high heat and pour over meat.

INGREDIENTS

4 1/2 pounds (2 kg) crabapples
1 cup (250 mL) water
2 1/2 cups (625 mL) sugar
1/4 cup (60 mL) cider vinegar
6 rosemary sprigs

METHOD

1. Combine whole apples and water and bring to a boil. Cook for 25 minutes, stirring and mashing the fruit often, or cook 2 minutes in the pressure cooker.

2. Pour fruit pulp into jelly bag or colander lined with cheesecloth and drain overnight.

3. Measure liquid and add a little water if necessary to make 3 cups (750 mL).

4. Combine juice, sugar, vinegar and rosemary. Bring slowly to a boil while stirring. Cook over high heat until jelly point is reached, about 15 minutes. Ladle into hot, sterilized jars and seal.

Makes 4 cups (1 L).

LIVER PÂTÉ WITH ROSEMARY JELLY

This smooth pâté has a delicate flavor with just a hint of sweetness. I serve it chilled, with toasted whole wheat bread.

INGREDIENTS

6 French shallots or 2 medium onions, minced
2 tbsp (30 mL) butter
1 pound (500 g) chicken livers, chopped
3 tbsp (45 mL) crabapple-rosemary jelly (see page 102)
salt and pepper

METHOD

1. Cook onions in butter until soft. Add livers and sauté 2 minutes.

2. Soften jelly in microwave or small pan. Add to livers, season to taste, cover and cook over moderate heat until done. The livers should stay pink inside.

3. Purée in food processor or blender until smooth.

4. Pour into crock and cool several hours before serving. Keeps one week, covered, in the refrigerator.

Makes about 2 cups (500 mL).

SUGARLESS PLUM JAM

So you are on a diet. That doesn't mean you have to suffer! Here, just for you, is a naturally sweetened jam.

INGREDIENTS

2 pounds (1 kg) Italian plums, pitted and chopped
1 can frozen apple juice concentrate

METHOD

1. Combine plums and apple juice concentrate. Cook uncovered over moderate heat until thick, about 1 hour.

2. Ladle into hot, sterilized jars and seal. Keep in the refrigerator, up to 3 months.

Makes 4 cups (1 L).

ORIENTAL PLUM SAUCE

Serve this sauce with egg rolls.

INGREDIENTS

1 cup (250 mL) sugarless plum jam
1/2 cup (125 mL) apple-carrot chutney (see page 115)
1/4 cup (60 mL) soy sauce
1 tbsp (15 mL) sesame oil
1 tbsp (15 mL) fresh ginger juice
1 tbsp (15 mL) lemon juice

METHOD

Combine ingredients and purée in blender or food processor.

Makes about 2 cups (500 mL).

PLUM MARMALADE WITH RUM

This marmalade makes a wonderful filling for *aumônières* (see page 29).

INGREDIENTS

2 oranges
1 cup (250 mL) water
2 pounds (1 kg) plums, pitted and chopped
3 cups (750 mL) sugar
1 cup (250 mL) pecans, coarsely chopped
1/2 cup (125 mL) rum or 3 tbsp (45 mL) rum extract

METHOD

1. Slice oranges thinly, removing pits. Soak overnight in water.

2. Combine oranges, water, plums and sugar. Bring to a boil while stirring. Cook over moderate heat until thick.

3. Add pecans and rum. Ladle into hot, sterilized jars and seal. Age one month minimum before using.

Makes 3 16-ounce (500 mL) jars.

ONION MARMALADE

Like candied shallots (see page 114), this sweet and sour marmalade is delicious with cold cuts, strong Cheddar-type cheeses and pork dishes.

INGREDIENTS

5 large onions, minced, about 6 cups (1.5 L)
1/2 cup (125 mL) oil
1 cup (250 mL) brown sugar
1/2 cup (125 mL) maple syrup
1/4 cup (60 mL) cider vinegar
1/2 tsp (2 mL) ground cloves
1/2 tsp (2 mL) ground coriander
1/2 tsp (2 mL) nutmeg

METHOD

1. Cook onions in oil 5 minutes while stirring. Add remaining ingredients and cook over moderate heat for 45 minutes or until thick.

2. Store in crock or glass jar in the refrigerator, up to 1 month.

Makes about 2 cups (500 mL).

CARROT-CINNAMON CAKE

During the reign of James I of England, it was fashionable for ladies to wear headdresses made of feathery carrot leaves.

INGREDIENTS

2 eggs
1 cup (250 mL) oil
1/2 cup (125 mL) brown sugar
1 cup (250 mL) or more carrot-cinnamon marmalade (see page 113)
1 cup (250 mL) orange juice
1 tbsp (15 mL) orange-blossom water (optional)
2 cups (500 mL) flour
1 1/2 tsp (7 mL) baking powder
1 1/2 tsp (7 mL) baking soda
pinch of salt

METHOD

1. Preheat oven to 375°F (190°C). Grease a 10-inch (26 cm) bundt pan.

2. In food processor, beat eggs and add oil in a slow, steady stream as you would for a mayonnaise. Add sugar, marmalade, orange juice and orange-blossom water.

3. Combine dry ingredients and fold in the egg mixture. Pour into the bundt pan. Cook 35 minutes or until a cake tester comes out clean.

Makes 8 to 10 portions.

Variation: Replace marmalade with butternut-maple butter (see page 146).

CARROT-CINNAMON MARMALADE

The cinnamon tree – the spice is the dried inner bark of the shoots – is a strange creature. It requires heat, constant rain, extremely poor soil (composed almost exclusively of sand) and a sheltered place to grow.

INGREDIENTS

4 cups (1 L) grated carrots
4 cups (1 L) orange juice
juice of 1 lemon
3 cups (750 mL) sugar
1 tsp (5 mL) cinnamon

METHOD

1. Cook carrots in orange juice over moderate heat for 30 minutes.

2. Add sugar and cinnamon. Stir thoroughly and cook until thick.

3. Ladle into hot, sterilized jars and seal.

Makes 3 cups (750 mL).

CANDIED SHALLOTS

Like garlic and onions, shallots are a member of the lily family. Sweeter than onions, they can be added raw to salads but are mainly used in sauces. A favorite condiment of French provincial cuisine, shallots are also popular in Oriental and Creole cooking.

INGREDIENTS

1 pound (500 g) shallots
1/2 cup (125 mL) maple syrup
1/4 cup (60 mL) water
salt and pepper

METHOD

1. Peel shallots. To make this easier, blanch them in boiling water for a few minutes.

2. Combine ingredients in heavy saucepan, season to taste and bring to a boil. Reduce heat and cook until the liquid forms a syrup.

3. Store in sealed crock or glass jar in the refrigerator. Keeps 3 to 4 weeks.

Makes about 1 1/2 (375 mL) cups.

APPLE-CARROT CHUTNEY

This chutney goes well with ham and roast pork. It also makes a delicious spread (see page 117) and is a key ingredient in Oriental plum sauce (see page 106).

INGREDIENTS

6 large cooking apples, peeled, cored and cubed, about 6 cups (1.5 L)
5 big carrots, coarsely grated (4 cups/1 L)
3 cups (750 mL) brown sugar
1 cup (250 mL) cider vinegar
1 cup (250 mL) raisins
1/3 cup (75 mL) minced fresh ginger
peel and juice of 1 orange
1/2 tsp (2 mL) each of: allspice, ground cloves, nutmeg
1/4 tsp (1 mL) ground pepper
1/4 tsp (1 mL) cayenne pepper or 1 hot chili pepper

METHOD

1. Combine all ingredients in heavy pot. Bring to a boil, then reduce heat and simmer 1 hour until thick, stirring frequently.

2. Ladle into hot, sterilized jars and seal. Keeps 6 months.

Makes about 5 cups (1.25 L).

CHUTNEY-CHEESE SPREAD

Chutney comes from *chatni*, meaning "hot spices" in Hindustani. However, chutney is not an original Indian recipe. It is a British specialty dating from colonial times.

INGREDIENTS

$^1/_2$ pound (250 g) cream cheese or 1 cup (250 mL) yogurt cheese (see page 67)
3 tbsp (45 mL) apple-carrot chutney (see page 115)

METHOD

Combine all ingredients and serve with toasted pita triangles.

Makes 1 cup (250 mL).

Variation: You may also add $^1/_2$ cup (125 mL) buttermilk or plain yogurt to make a delicious dip for raw vegetables.

INDIAN CHUTNEY

Ginger makes an attractive houseplant. Pick a firm, shiny rhizome, preferably one showing a bud. Fill a large pot with a light potting mix. Plant the root close to the surface with part of the bud showing. Keep in a warm, sunny spot and water frequently. The first shoot may take up to a month to show but don't be discouraged. You will soon see other bamboo-like shoots spring from the root.

Put the ginger plant outdoors in the summer in a shady spot and water regularly. Fertilize once a month, using an organic fertilizer if you wish to eat the root. To harvest, simply cut a piece of the fleshy root with a sharp, clean knife.

I must confess I have never been able to do that. What! Mutilate a plant I have so lovingly grown? Certainly not! I buy ginger at the market and keep my plant whole and happy.

INGREDIENTS

2 cups (500 mL) dried figs, chopped
3 1/2 cups (875 mL) dates, chopped
1 1/2 cup (375 mL) raisins
2 each of: green and red bell peppers, seeded and chopped
2 large onions, chopped
3 garlic cloves, minced
1 3/4-inch (2 cm) piece fresh ginger
5 cups (1.25L) cider vinegar
3 cups (750 mL) brown sugar
2 tbsp (30 mL) pickling salt
3 tbsp (45 mL) curry powder (see page 81)
1/2 tsp (2 mL) ground pepper
1 tsp (5 mL) ground cloves
2 mangos or papayas, chopped
grated peel and juice of 2 lemons and 2 oranges
1/2 cup (125 mL) sherry
1/3 cup (75 mL) slivered almonds

Method

1. Combine dried fruits, vegetables, ginger, vinegar, sugar, salt and spices in heavy pot. Simmer 1 hour, stirring frequently.

2. Add remaining fruit, grated peel and juice of the lemons and oranges and simmer another hour. Add sherry and almonds and cook 10 more minutes.

3. Ladle into hot, sterilized jars. Age 2 months before using. Keeps one year or more.

Makes 7 ½ 16-ounce (500 mL) jars.

CHICKEN WITH INDIAN CHUTNEY

Like curries and chutneys, ketchup (from the Siamese *kachiap*) originated in Asia. In 1837, American companies wanting to sell ketchup in Britain were advised to call it tomato chutney, since ketchup already referred to a sauce made with anchovies or mushrooms.

INGREDIENTS

2 chicken breasts
1 medium onion, minced
1 garlic clove, minced
cooking oil
1 tbsp (15 mL) curry powder (see page 81)
1 cup (250 mL) Indian chutney (see page 118)
1 tbsp (15 mL) corn starch
1/2 cup (15 mL) water

METHOD

1. Remove any skin, bone and fat from chicken breasts. Cut into cubes.

2. Sauté onion in oil. Sprinkle with curry powder and cook 1 minute. Add chicken and sear on all sides.

3. Add chutney, mix well, cover and simmer 5 minutes.

4. Dilute corn starch in water. Add to chicken and let thicken over medium heat. Serve with saffron rice.

Makes 2 portions.

SALSA PIQUANTE

To preserve the flavor of fresh tomatoes, I keep the cooking time to a minimum and remove the excess liquid by using a small strainer to ladle the salsa into jars. I use the leftover juice in sauces or as cooking liquid for rice.

INGREDIENTS

5 1/2 pounds (2.5 kg) tomatoes, peeled, seeded and coarsely chopped
2 large onions, chopped
2 green bell peppers, seeded and chopped
3 red bell peppers, seeded and chopped
4 chili peppers, seeded and chopped
1 or 2 garlic cloves, minced
1/2 cup(125 mL) cider vinegar
1/4 cup (60 mL) sugar
2 tbsp (30 mL) pickling salt
1 tsp (2 mL) paprika
grated peel and juice of 2 limes
3 tbsp (45 mL) fresh coriander seeds, crushed

METHOD

1. Combine all ingredients, except lime and coriander. Bring to a boil, while stirring.

2. Cook over high heat for 15 to 20 minutes, until thick. Add lime and coriander, stir well and cook another minute.

3. Ladle into hot, sterilized jars and seal. Or freeze.

Makes about 14 cups (3.5 L).

GRILLED SHRIMP

INGREDIENTS

jumbo shrimp
Cajun spices (see page 76)
salsa piquante (see page 123)

METHOD

Peel and devein shrimp. Sprinkle with spices and barbecue or grill. Serve with salsa piquante.

MUSSELS MARINESCA

This is one of my favorite ways to prepare mussels.

INGREDIENTS

2 pounds (1 kg) mussels
1 carrot, sliced
1 celery stalk, chopped
¼ cup (125 mL) white wine
½ cup (125 mL) salsa piquante (see page 123)
fresh coriander

METHOD

1. Combine carrot, celery and wine in a large saucepan. Bring to a boil.

2. Add mussels, cover and cook over medium-high heat for 5 minutes, until mussels are open, shaking the pan a couple of times.

3. Discard any mussels that have stayed closed. Add salsa, heat thoroughly and serve sprinkled with fresh coriander.

Makes 4 portions.

FRUIT SALSA

Dried coriander seeds lose the pungent smell and taste of the fresh plant and acquire a delicate citrus flavor that goes well in cakes, biscuits and sweet and sour dishes.

INGREDIENTS

4 1/2 pounds (2 kg) tomatoes, peeled, seeded and chopped, about 6 cups (1.5 L)
5 peaches, peeled and chopped
5 pears, peeled and chopped
5 tart apples, peeled and chopped
7 celery stalks, chopped
5 onions, minced
3 to 6 hot chili peppers, seeded and chopped
2 cups (500 mL) cider vinegar
2 cups (500 mL) brown sugar
2 tbsp (30 mL) pickling salt
2 tbsp (30 mL) dried coriander seeds, crushed
1 tsp (5 mL) paprika

METHOD

1. Combine all ingredients and bring slowly to a boil, while stirring.

2. Simmer, uncovered, for 1 hour or until thick. Stir frequently to prevent sticking.

3. Ladle into hot, sterilized jars and seal.

Makes about 12 cups (3 L).

SHARK CAJUN STYLE

To successfully "blacken" fish or meat Cajun-style, the frying pan must be extremely hot. Use a cast-iron pan for best results.

INGREDIENTS

1 pound (500 g) shark fillets
1 tbsp (30 mL) Cajun spices (see page 76)
1 cup (250 mL) fruit salsa (see page 129)
1/4 cup (60 mL) cooking oil
grated peel and juice of 1 lime

METHOD

1. Cut fillets into strips or cubes and sprinkle with Cajun spices.

2. Heat pan several minutes before pouring in the oil. Add shark pieces immediately and sear on all sides. Add salsa and lime juice, reduce heat, cover and cook 3 to 5 minutes.

3. Sprinkle with grated lime peel and serve with wild rice or rice and beans.

Makes 4 portions

Tip: Fillets from small shark are more tender than those from big shark.

CHINESE PICKLES

Also called mirlitons, chayotes are a type of climbing squash, producing green, furrowed pear-shaped fruits. The meat is white, firm and sweet. It is eaten raw in salad or cooked. An ingredient of accras, Caribbean fritters made with salt cod, the chayote is also used in Oriental cooking and the best place to buy them is an Asian grocery store.

INGREDIENTS

2 carrots
2 chayotes
2 kohlrabi
4 celery stalks
1 red bell pepper

Brine
1/3 cup (75 mL) ginger, peeled and chopped
2 star anise
2 cloves
3 cups (750 mL) sugar
3 cups (750 mL) white vinegar
1 1/2 cups (375 mL) water
1 tsp (5 mL) salt

METHOD

1. Combine ingredients of the brine and dissolve sugar over low heat, while stirring. Bring to a boil, remove from heat and cool.

2. Cut vegetables in sticks. Blanch 2 minutes in boiling water and let dry 1 hour on towel.

3. Pack vegetables in large glass or stoneware jar and pour brine over them. Store in the refrigerator for 1 week before using. Keeps 3 months.

Makes 8 cups (2 L).

CURRIED GREEN TOMATO SAUCE

So you planted too many tomato plants. Well, here is one way to use the green ones.

INGREDIENTS

3 pounds (1.5 kg) cubed green tomatoes, about 6 cups (1.5 L)
2 onions, coarsely chopped
1/4 cup butter
4 tbsp (60 mL) curry powder (see page 81)
1 tbsp (15 mL) ground cumin
1 cup (250 mL) water or coconut milk
1/2 cup (125 mL) brown sugar
1/2 cup (125 mL) raisins
2 tbsp (30 mL) lemon juice
salt to taste

METHOD

1. Sauté onions in butter until soft. Sprinkle with curry powder and cook 3 minutes. Add remaining ingredients and simmer 30 minutes, stirring occasionally. Add more water if necessary.

2. Ladle into jars, seal and process in boiling water for 30 minutes or 10 minutes in the pressure cooker. Or freeze.

3. Serve on bed of rice, with grilled chicken or fish.

Makes 5 16-ounce (500 mL) jars.

WINTER

BANANA-PRUNE COMPOTE

This compote makes a quick and nutritious breakfast as well as a healthy and refreshing dessert.

INGREDIENTS

1 cup (250 mL) pitted prunes
1 cup (250 mL) pineapple juice
4 medium apples, peeled and cored
1 banana
dash of each: cinnamon, vanilla

METHOD

1. Soak prunes in pineapple juice for several hours or soften over low heat.

2. Purée fruits in blender or food processor. Combine with vanilla and cinnamon and cook over low heat until thick, stirring frequently.

3. Ladle into jar and seal. Store in the refrigerator for up to 1 month.

Makes about 1 $1/2$ cups (375 mL).

WINTER FRUIT COMPOTE

INGREDIENTS

2 cups (500 mL) cooking dates
1 cup (250 mL) pineapple juice
3 pears
5 apples
1/2 cup (125 mL) cooked butternut squash (optional)

METHOD

1. Soak dates, pears, apples and squash (optional) in pineapple juice for several hours or soften over low heat.

2. Purée fruits in blender or food processor. Cook over low heat until thick, stirring frequently.

3. Ladle into jars and seal. Store in the refrigerator for up to 1 month.

Makes about 4 cups (1 L).

QUICKIE BREAKFAST OR DESSERT

INGREDIENTS

1 cup (250 mL) ricotta or cottage cheese
2 tbsp (30 mL) banana-prune or winter fruit compote (see page 138)
Pears in pineapple juice (see page 96)
1 tbsp (15 mL) slivered almonds, optional

METHOD

Combine cheese and compote. Arrange on serving plates surrounded by pear slices. Sprinkle with almonds.

ORANGE-PARSNIP MARMALADE

The 16th century English botanist John Gerard wrote this about the lowly parsnip. "There is a good, pleasant food or bread made of the roots of the parsnip, which I have myself not tried yet, nor mean to." If he had known how good parsnips can taste....

INGREDIENTS

4 oranges
3 cups (750 mL) water
4 cups (1 L) parsnips, grated
2 cups (500 mL) orange juice
4 cups (1 L) sugar

METHOD

1. Cut oranges in half and slice thinly, removing pits. Soak in water overnight.

2. Combine all ingredients. Dissolve sugar over low heat, then bring to a boil. Cook until thick, about 35 to 40 minutes, stirring frequently.

3. Ladle into hot, sterilized jars and seal.

Makes 8 cups (2 L).

CARROT-PARSNIP COMPOTE

Creamy and sweet, this compote makes a great spread when mixed with cream cheese, and combined with cottage or ricotta cheese it makes a tasty dessert or breakfast. You can also use it as a filling for danishes or other pastries, or make it into a mousse, like the maple mousse made with butternut-maple butter (see page 146).

INGREDIENTS

2 pounds (1 kg) carrots
1 pound (500 g) parsnips
2 cups (500 mL) orange juice
2 cups (500 mL) maple syrup

METHOD

1. Cook carrots and parsnips in orange juice until very tender. Purée in blender or food processor.

2. Combine with maple syrup and cook over moderate heat until thick.

3. Ladle into hot, sterilized jars and seal. Store in refrigerator and use within 2 months or freeze for up to 1 year.

Makes about 8 cups (2 L).

SOUFFLÉ PIE

The quick preparation of this light dessert makes up for the long baking time.

INGREDIENTS

3 eggs, separated
1 1/2 cups (375 mL) carrot-parsnip compote (see page 143)
1 9-inch (23 cm) pie shell

METHOD

1. Preheat oven to 375°F (190°C).

2. Beat egg yolks until fluffy, then add compote. Whip egg whites until stiff and fold into the mixture.

3. Pour into pie shell and bake for 1 1/4 hours or until a cake tester comes out clean.

Makes 6 to 8 portions.

BUTTERNUT-MAPLE BUTTER

I call this the poor man's *crème de marrons* because it is made with common, inexpensive ingredients and tastes very much like the famous and costly French chestnut cream.

INGREDIENTS

butternut squash
water
maple syrup
vanilla

METHOD

1. Peel squash, remove seeds and filaments and cut into cubes. Steam or cook in a little water until very tender. Purée in blender or food processor.

2. Measure pulp and for every 4 cups (1 L), use 1 cup (250 mL) of maple syrup and 1 tsp (5 mL) of vanilla. Combine all ingredients and bring to a boil. Reduce heat and simmer until thick, stirring frequently. To reduce splashing, cover pot with wire mesh.

3. Ladle into hot, sterilized jars and seal or freeze. Keeps in refrigerator for 2 months or up to one year in the freezer.

MAPLE MOUSSE

Like all winter squash, butternut is rich in vitamins and minerals. Just half a cup provides the total daily requirements of vitamin A.

INGREDIENTS

1 cup (250 mL) whipping cream
1 cup (250 mL) butternut-maple butter (see page 146)
slivered almonds, roasted, to garnish

METHOD

1. Whip cream until soft peaks are formed. Fold compote delicately into whipped cream.

2. Pour into tall glasses or a cooked pie shell, sprinkle with roasted slivered almonds and chill.

Makes 4 portions.

CANDIED GINGER

I have many uses for this sweet yet pungent candy. I serve it after a rich meal to help digestion. I nibble on it while cross-country skiing for warmth and energy. And I add it chopped to fruit cakes. If there is any left – not too often, I might add – and it becomes hard, I grind it in the blender and use it to flavor cakes and muffins.

INGREDIENTS

1/2 cup (125 mL) very fresh ginger
1/2 cup (125 mL) water
1/2 cup (125 mL) sugar

METHOD

1. Peel and slice ginger. Cover with water, bring to a boil, then simmer for 15 minutes. Drain. Reserve liquid for baking and Oriental dishes.

2. In heavy saucepan, dissolve sugar in 1/2 cup (125 mL) water. Bring to a boil and add ginger. Reduce heat and simmer until sugar is absorbed.

3. Roll ginger pieces in sugar and store in tight container. It will keep soft for a month or two if it's kept in a sealed jar or tin.

TURNIP-BUTTERNUT FLANS

When I serve these delicate flans, my guests are always surprised to find they are eating the dreaded turnip.

INGREDIENTS

1 cup (250 mL) puréed turnip
¹/2 cup (125 mL) butternut-maple butter (see page 146)
3 eggs
salt and pepper
butter

METHOD

1. Combine turnip purée and butternut-maple butter. Beat in eggs, one at a time. Season with salt and pepper to taste.

2. Pour into buttered ramekins and cook in microwave, at medium, for 10 minutes. Or set dishes in ³/4 inch (2 cm) of water and bake at 375° F (190° C) for 15 to 20 minutes until centers are firm.

Makes 4 portions.

MOCHA CAKE

Mocha is a variety of coffee bean first grown in Arabia. It is also the name of a dessert made with layers of sponge cake and butter cream, flavored with coffee and chocolate. Over time, mocha came to mean the combination of these two flavors.

INGREDIENTS

1 cup (250 mL) hazelnuts
4 eggs
1 cup (250 mL) sugar
1 tbsp (15 mL) baking powder
1/2 cup (125 mL) flour
1/4 cup (60 mL) cocoa powder
1 tbsp (15 mL) instant coffee

Filling
1 cup (250 mL) whipping cream
1 cup (250 mL) butternut-maple butter (see page 146)

METHOD

1. Line bottoms of three 9-inch (1 L) round cake pans with parchment or waxed paper. Grease and set aside.

2. Spread hazelnuts on baking sheet. Bake in 350°F (180°C) oven for 8 minutes. Transfer to tea towel. Fold towel over nuts and rub off skins. In food processor or blender, chop hazelnuts finely.

3. In large bowl with electric mixer, beat eggs with sugar for 10 minutes (not less) until thick and pale in color. Combine dry ingredients and fold delicately into egg mixture.

4. Pour batter into prepared pans and bake for 20 to 25 minutes until cake tester comes out clean. Cool 5 minutes before turning out on a rack. Remove paper and cool completely.

5. Whip cream. Fold in butternut-maple butter. Spread 1/3 of the filling on one cake, top with another layer and repeat. For the last layer of cream, use a piping bag to decorate the top of the cake.

Makes 6 to 8 portions.

ORANGE AND SPICE MARMALADE

Marmalade comes from the Portuguese word *marmelada*, which originally referred to quince jam. In the 1790s, a Scotsman from Dundee created the first orange marmalade as we know it today. But according to one fanciful account, marmalade was created by Mary Queen of Scots' physician. He allegedly mixed oranges and sugar to alleviate his royal patient's seasickness, and the name comes from the phrase, *"Marie est malade"* (Mary is sick).

INGREDIENTS

8 oranges
2 lemons
water
9 cups (2.25L) sugar, approximately
1 tsp (15 mL) ground cloves
1 small stick cinnamon
1 star anise
1 walnut-size piece of ginger

METHOD

1. Cut oranges and lemons in half lengthwise, then in thin slices, removing pits. Measure and add 1 1/2 cups water for each cup of fruit. Soak overnight.

2. Measure again and for every cup, use 3/4 cup (185 mL) sugar. Set sugar aside.

3. Bring fruit and water to a boil and cook 20 minutes. Add sugar, and the spices tied in cheesecloth. Cook until thick.

4. Remove spice bag and ladle marmalade into hot, sterilized jars. Seal.

Makes about 6 cups (1.5 L).

Tip: This marmalade can be used to make a wonderfully flavored salad dressing. Simply whisk together 1/2 cup (125 mL) olive oil, 1 tbsp (15 mL) lemon juice, 2 tbsp (30 mL) orange and spice marmalade, and salt and pepper to taste. Pour over sliced beet, orange and endive salad.

MARMALADE BUNS

Even if I give away most of my preserves, I always end up with more jams and marmalades than I can eat on toast. So I make these scrumptious buns.

INGREDIENTS

1 tsp (5 mL) sugar
1/2 cup (125 mL) warm water
1 package active dry yeast
1 cup (250 mL) milk
2 tbsp (30 mL) butter
1 tbsp (15 mL) orange-blossom water (optional)
3 eggs
4 cups (1 L) flour
2 tbsp (30 mL) sugar
pinch of salt

Filling
1 cup (250 mL) marmalade or jam of your choice
1/2 cup (125 mL) pine nuts or pecans

METHOD

1. Dissolve yeast in warm water with 1 tsp (5 mL) sugar.

2. Heat milk with butter and if desired flavor with orange-blossom water. Remove from heat and beat in eggs.

3. Sift together dry ingredients. Add dissolved yeast and egg mixture and knead until dough is elastic.

4. Place dough in greased bowl, cover and let rise in a warm place until double in size (1 to 2 hours).

5. Soften marmalade in microwave or in small pan. Add nuts and mix.

6. Punch down dough and roll out into a 16 x 12-inch (40 x 30 cm) square. Spread with marmalade-nut filling and roll lengthwise. Cut in 16 pieces and arrange in a buttered baking pan. Let rise 1 hour.

7. Brush tops of buns with some marmalade diluted in water and then bake at 375° F (190° C) for 25 minutes.

Makes 16 buns.

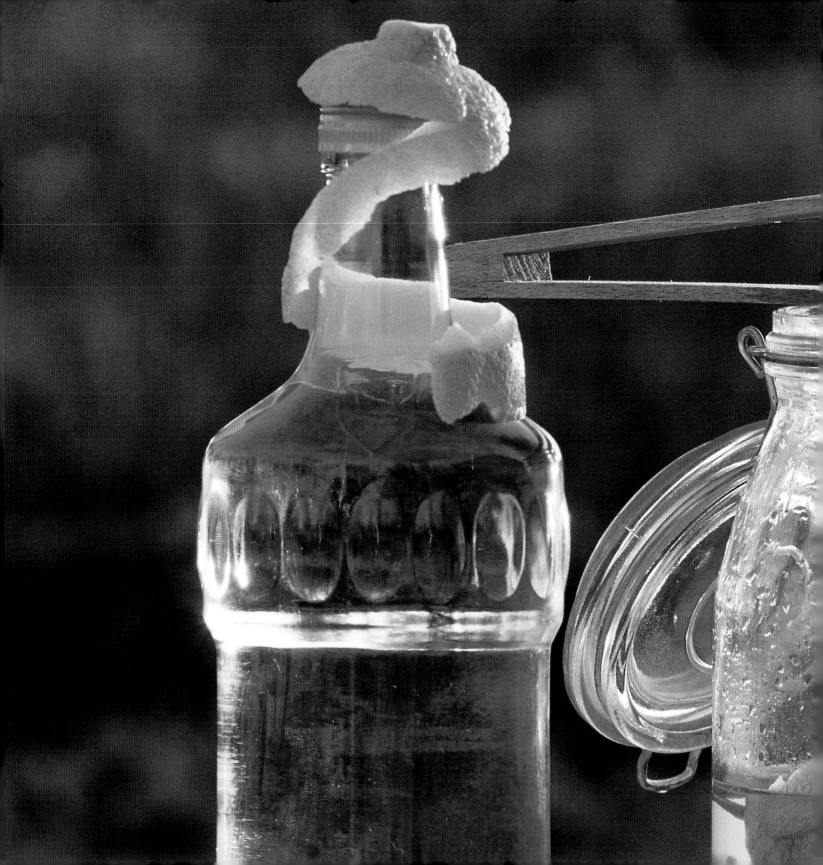

ORANGE RATAFIA

Use organic fruits for this aperitif, since washing and brushing citrus skins does not remove all chemicals. In fact, I recommend that you buy organic fruits and vegetables for all your preserves. If you can afford them, of course!

INGREDIENTS

6 oranges
2 lemons
2 cups (500 mL) vodka
6 cups (1.5 L) dry white wine
1 1/2 cup (375 mL) cup sugar

METHOD

1. Peel fruit, removing as little of the white membrane as possible. Place peel in glass container, pour vodka over and seal. Set aside for 6 weeks.

2. Strain alcohol and discard citrus peels.

3. Add wine and sugar to alcohol, stirring until sugar is dissolved. Strain again if cloudy. Bottle, seal and age for 6 months. Frankly, I have never been able to wait that long!

Makes 8 cups (2 L).

CANDIED CITRUS PEELS

The word grapefruit was used for the first time in 1814 by John Lunan, an English botanist, who developed the fruit from the Polynesian pomelo tree. For tender candied peels, choose fruit with thick skin.

INGREDIENTS

3 oranges
3 grapefruit
4 1/2 cups (1.25 L) sugar
1 cup (250 mL) water

METHOD

1. Cut fruit in quarters. Detach pulp from skin by pulling sides apart and lifting it off.

2. Cut skin in strips 1/4 inch (5 mm) wide. Cook in boiling water for 30 minutes. Drain and cool.

3. In heavy saucepan, dissolve sugar in 1 cup (250 mL) of water over medium heat. Add peels and cook until sugar is absorbed, about 20 minutes.

4. With tongs, remove peels and roll in sugar. Dry on a rack overnight. Store in tight container. Keeps 2 to 3 weeks.

SOUTH SEAS BANANAS

Whip up this quick dessert for Valentine's Day and have more time to spend with your loved one.

INGREDIENTS

2 bananas, not too ripe
1 tbsp (15 mL) hazelnut oil or unsalted butter
2 tbsp (30 mL) South Seas marmalade (see page 164)
sour cream

METHOD

1. Peel and cut bananas diagonally.

2. Heat oil or butter and sauté bananas for 1 minute, turning pieces delicately with spoon.

3. Add marmalade and heat a few seconds.

4. Serve warm with sour cream.

Makes 2 portions.

SOUTH SEAS MARMALADE

Don't be too quick to taste this marmalade. Let time work its magic.
After one year, the flavors will blend into a rich taste, with an almost
candied texture.

INGREDIENTS

1 lemon
1 orange
1 lime
2 cups (500 mL) water
1 ripe pineapple, chopped, about 3 cups (750 mL)
3 cups (750 mL) pure cane sugar
1/2 tsp (2 mL) allspice
1/2 cup (125 mL) rum or 1 tbsp (15 mL) rum flavoring (see page 165)

METHOD

1. Slice citrus fruit thinly, removing pits. Soak in water overnight.

2. Combine all ingredients except rum and bring to a boil. Reduce heat and
   simmer until thick. Add rum.

3. Ladle into hot, sterilized jars and seal.

Makes 4 cups.

PINEAPPLE-GINGER MARMALADE

Ripe pineapple has small black seeds embedded in the flesh. Because they are hard to remove when peeling the fruit, I use the tip of a sharp knife to take them out one by one while the marmalade is cooking .

INGREDIENTS

1 ripe pineapple, chopped, about 3 cups (750 mL)
2 cups (500 mL) sugar
grated peel and juice of 2 limes
1 tbsp (15 mL) minced fresh ginger

METHOD

1. Combine pineapple, sugar and lime peel in heavy saucepan and cook until thick, about 15 to 20 minutes. Add lime juice and ginger.

2. Ladle into hot, sterilized jars and seal.

Makes about 3 cups (750 mL).

Tip: Mix any leftover pineapple pulp with cottage or ricotta cheese for a refreshing dessert, or freeze and make naturally sweetened slush by whipping frozen pulp with a little water in a blender.

ORANGE-CRANBERRY MARMALADE

In my kitchen, this marmalade has one use and one use only, to make Duck à l'Orange (see page 169).

INGREDIENTS

3 oranges
1 cup (250 mL) water
3 cups (750 mL) cranberries
3 cups (750 mL) sugar
1 cup (250 mL) orange juice

METHOD

1. Slice oranges thinly, removing pits. Soak in water overnight.

2. Coarsely chop cranberries. Combine ingredients in a heavy saucepan and bring to a boil. Cook over medium heat for 25 minutes until thick.

3. Ladle into hot, sterilized jars and seal.

Makes 2 16-ounce (500 mL) jars.

DUCK À L'ORANGE

Oranges are used extensively in French cooking, with fish, poultry and veal, and in sauces and salads.

INGREDIENTS

1 duck, 3 to 4 pounds (1.5 to 2 kg)
1 cup (250 mL) orange-cranberry marmalade (see page 167)
salt and pepper

METHOD

1. Remove breasts and legs of duck. Arrange on baking pan and set aside.

2. Grill carcass under the broiler, turning frequently until crisp and golden, about 15 minutes. Chop bones. Put in pan and cover with water. Bring to a boil and reduce until 1 cup of liquid is left. Strain.

3. Combine marmalade and liquid, pour over duck pieces, season to taste, cover with aluminium foil and bake at 375°F (190° C) for 45 minutes or until done.

4. Serve breasts sliced and legs whole, covered with remaining sauce.

Makes 4 to 6 portions.

INDEX